FORCES IN MOTION

PUSHING AND PULLING

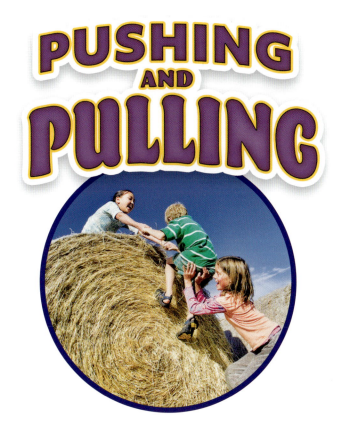

by Spencer Brinker

Consultant: Beth Gambro
Reading Specialist, Yorkville, Illinois

Minneapolis, Minnesota

Teaching Tips

Before Reading

- Look at the cover of the book. Discuss the picture and the title.
- Ask readers to brainstorm a list of what they already know about pushing and pulling. What can they expect to see in this book?
- Go on a picture walk, looking through the pictures to discuss vocabulary and make predictions about the text.

During Reading

- Read for purpose. As they are reading, encourage readers to think about pushing or pulling in their own lives.
- Ask readers to look for the details of the book. What are they learning about the things that cause movement?
- If readers encounter an unknown word, ask them to look at the sounds in the word. Then, ask them to look at the rest of the page. Are there any clues to help them understand?

After Reading

- Encourage readers to pick a buddy and reread the book together.
- Ask readers to name two things from the book that they can push or pull. Find the pages that tell about these things.
- Ask readers to write or draw something they learned about pushing and pulling.

Credits: Cover and title page, © Zia Soleil/Getty; 3, © LUHUANFENG/iStock; 4,5, © ssj414/iStock, © Chris Howey/Shutterstock, © Morinka/Shutterstock, © Yaisomanang/Shutterstock; 7, © jarenwicklund/Shutterstock; 9, © andresr/iStock; 11, © Erickson Stock/Shutterstock; 12,13, © mbbirdy/iStock; 14,15, © mixetto/iStock; 16, © yaoinlove/iStock; 17, © YAKOBCHUK VIACHESLAV/Shutterstock; 18,19, © SolStock/iStock; 20,21, © Andersen Ross Photography Inc/Getty; 22T, © kozmoat98/iStock; 22B, © Bogdanhoda/iStock; 23TL, © BraunS/iStock; 23TM, © Smileus/Shutterstock; 23TR, © GOLFX/Shutterstock; 23BL, © alexei_tm/Shutterstock; 23BM, © Boris Medvedev/Shutterstock; 23BL, © _jure/iStock.

Library of Congress Cataloging-in-Publication Data

Names: Brinker, Spencer, author.
Title: Pushing and pulling / by Spencer Brinker.
Description: Bearcub books. | Minneapolis, Minnesota : Bearport Publishing
  Company, [2022] | Series: Forces in motion | Includes bibliographical
  references and index.
Identifiers: LCCN 2021045086 (print) | LCCN 2021045087 (ebook) | ISBN
  9781636914114 (library binding) | ISBN 9781636914169 (paperback) | ISBN
  9781636914213 (ebook)
Subjects: LCSH: Force and energy--Juvenile literature. | Motion--Juvenile
  literature.
Classification: LCC QC73.4 .B76 2022 (print) | LCC QC73.4 (ebook) | DDC
  531.6--dc23
LC record available at https://lccn.loc.gov/2021045086
LC ebook record available at https://lccn.loc.gov/2021045087

Copyright © 2022 Bearport Publishing Company. All rights reserved. No part of this publication may be reproduced in whole or in part, stored in any retrieval system, or transmitted in any form or by any means, electronic, mechanical, photocopying, recording, or otherwise, without written permission from the publisher.

For more information, write to Bearport Publishing, 5357 Penn Avenue South, Minneapolis, MN 55419. Printed in the United States of America.

Contents

Let's Move It! 4

Machines that Push and Pull 22

Glossary 23

Index 24

Read More 24

Learn More Online 24

About the Author 24

Let's Move It!

Uff!

This pumpkin is **heavy**!

How can we move it?

My dog can pull in front.

I can push from the back.

Pulling means bringing something to you.

To go outside, you can use the door.

You pull the handle to open it.

Happy Birthday!

Your present has a big bow.

Pull the ribbon to take it off.

Hold its end and bring the ribbon to you.

Pushing is when you make something go away from you.

You can push your sister on a swing.

It makes her go so high.

Whoosh!

Look at that boat go.

How does it move?

The wind pushes it!

Pushing and pulling are **forces**.

They make things move.

They need **energy** to do it.

You only need a little energy to push the button.

But the bag is heavy.

You need a lot of energy to pull it.

Sometimes, two forces are **balanced**.

Energy coming from **opposite** sides is the same.

Forces make motion all around.

Every day we move things.

What have you pushed or pulled today?

Machines that Push and Pull

Sometimes, we need lots of energy to push or pull things. Machines can help when we do not have the force to do it ourselves.

A tow truck pulls heavy cars.

A **bulldozer** pushes a lot of dirt.

Glossary

balanced equal

bulldozer a truck that moves dirt

energy a measure of how much work something can do

forces pushes or pulls that make things move

heavy large in size and weight

opposite on either side of something

Index

balanced 18
energy 14, 16, 18, 22
force 14, 18, 20, 22
heavy 4, 16, 22
opposite 18
pull 5–6, 8, 14, 16, 20, 22
push 5, 10, 13–14, 16, 20, 22

Read More

Duling, Kaitlyn. *Push and Pull (My Physical Science Library).* North Mankato, MN: Rourke Educational Media, 2020.

Lindeen, Mary. *Push and Pull (Beginning-to-Read: Physical Science).* Chicago: Norwood House Press, 2022.

Learn More Online

1. Go to **www.factsurfer.com** or scan the QR code below.
2. Enter "**Pushing and Pulling**" into the search box.
3. Click on the cover of this book to see a list of websites.

About the Author

Spencer Brinker lives in Minnesota with his family. Sometimes their dog, Linzer, seems to push and pull at the same time!